anythink

Safari Sam's Wild Animals

Mountain Animals

A⁺

Smart Apple Media

Published by Smart Apple Media, an imprint of Black Rabbit Books
P.O. Box 3263, Mankato, Minnesota 56002
www.smartapplemedia.com

Produced by David West Children's Books
6 Princeton Court, 55 Felsham Road, London SW15 1AZ

Designed and illustrated by David West

Copyright © 2014 David West Children's Books

Cataloging-in-Publication Data is available from
Library of Congress
ISBN 978-1-62588-073-4

Printed in China
CPSIA compliance information: DWCB15CP
311214

9 8 7 6 5 4 3 2 1

Safari Sam says:
I will tell you something
more about the animal.

Learn what this
animal eats.

Where in the
world is the
animal found?

Its size is revealed!

What animal group
is it—mammal, bird,
reptile, amphibian,
insect, or something
else?

Interesting facts.

Contents

Bighorn Sheep

Bighorn sheep are a type of mountain sheep. They are named after the large, curved horns of the male sheep called rams. They live in large flocks in alpine meadows, on grassy mountain slopes, and on foothills near rocky cliffs.

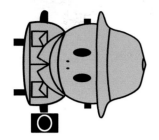

Safari Sam says:
Bighorn rams often fight each other during the mating season. They run at each other and crash into one another with their horns.

Bighorn sheep graze on grasses and shrubs.

 Most bighorn sheep live in the cooler mountain regions of Canada and the United States.

 Bighorns grow 6 feet (1.8 meters) long from the nose to the tail and weigh up to 300 pounds (140 kilograms).

 Bighorn sheep are mammals.

 Bighorns are expert at climbing steep terrain where they are safer from predators, such as bears, wolves, and cougars.

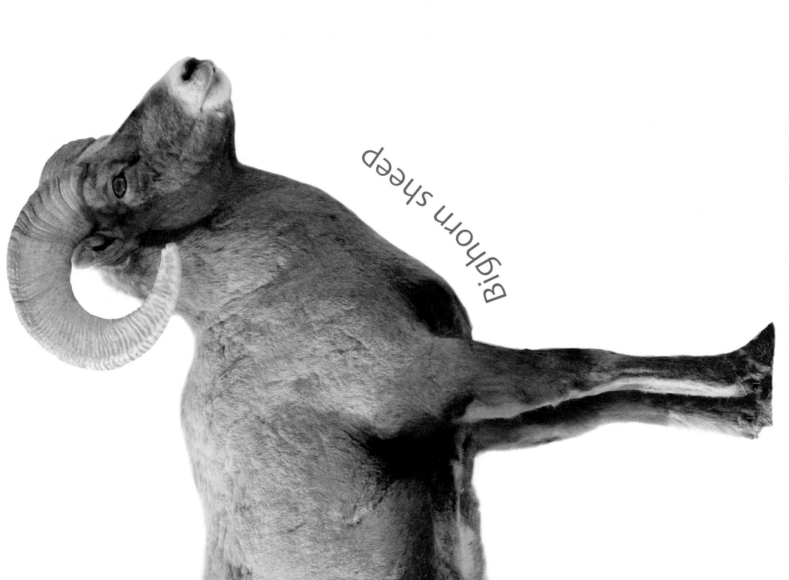

Bighorn sheep

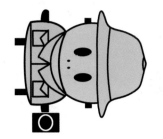

Chinchillas

Chinchillas are **rodents**. They live in social groups called herds. They were once hunted by humans for their extremely soft fur. In the wild, chinchillas are hunted by birds of prey, skunks, and snakes.

Safari Sam says:
To escape predators, chinchillas can jump up to 6 feet (1.8 meters). Their other escape tactics include spraying urine and releasing fur when bitten.

Chinchillas are not able to sweat. If temperatures rise above 80 °F (27 °C), they could overheat. They use their ears as radiators to get rid of excess body heat.

 Chinchillas are rodents, which are a type of mammal.

 Chinchillas are about 12 inches (30 centimeters) long.

 Chinchillas live at high altitudes, about 15,000 feet (4,500 meters), in the Andes Mountains in South America.

 Chinchillas eat plant leaves, fruits, seeds, and small insects.

Chinchilla

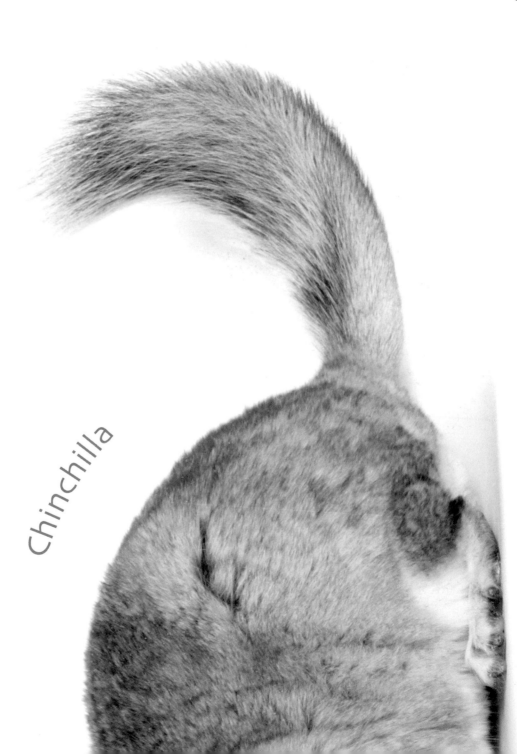

Condors

Condors are very large, broad-winged soaring birds. They have bald heads and a ruff of white feathers that surround the base of their necks.

Condors glide on updrafts of the mountain air and use their excellent eyesight to look for animal **carcasses** to eat.

The California condor's wingspan measures up to 9.5 feet (2.9 meters). The Andean condor's wingspan can measure over 10 feet (3 meters).

Condors are members of the vulture group of birds.

The Andean condor lives in the Andes Mountains of South America. The California condor lives in the western coastal mountains of Mexico and the United States.

The Andean condor is one of the world's longest-living birds. It can reach 70 years of age or more when living in zoos.

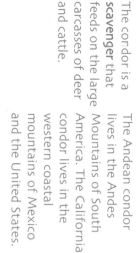

The condor is a **scavenger** that feeds on the large carcasses of deer and cattle.

Andean condor

Safari Sam says:
Condors have large territories and often travel 160 miles (250 kilometers) a day in search of food.

Golden Eagles

Most golden eagles live in mountainous regions. Many hunt and nest on rock formations. They use their powerful feet and sharp talons to snatch prey, such as hares and rabbits. Golden eagles have hooked beaks to tear the meat from the bodies of their prey.

Golden eagles hunt and eat the local prey of their hunting area. Their prey may include hares, ground squirrels, and game birds, such as grouse.

Golden eagles are found in Europe, North Africa, Asia, and North America.

Golden eagles can grow up to 3.25 feet (1 meter) in length and up to 7.5 feet (2.3 meters) in wingspan.

Golden eagles are birds of prey known for their hunting skills.

A golden eagle's nest is called an eyrie. They might build several eyries within their territory.

Safari Sam says:
During courtship, golden eagles may pick up a rock, drop it, and then fly in a steep dive to catch the falling rock in midair.

Golden eagle

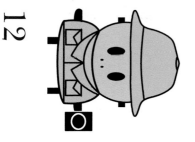

Ibexes

Ibexes are a type of wild goat that live in the mountains. Agile and hardy animals, they are able to climb on steep mountainsides and survive on little vegetation. The males have large, curved horns that they use to fight other males during the mating season.

Safari Sam says:
Ibexes are known for their great climbing ability. They have been seen standing on the steep face of a water dam licking the salt off of the stonework.

Ibexes mainly eat grasses and leaves.

Ibexes are found in Europe, the Middle East, Asia, and some parts of Africa.

Ibexes can grow up to 5.5 feet (1.7 meters) long with horns about 3.25 feet (1 meter) long.

Ibexes are mammals.

The ibex's coat is light, smooth, and shiny. It reflects a large amount of sunlight, which keeps it cool during the heat of summer.

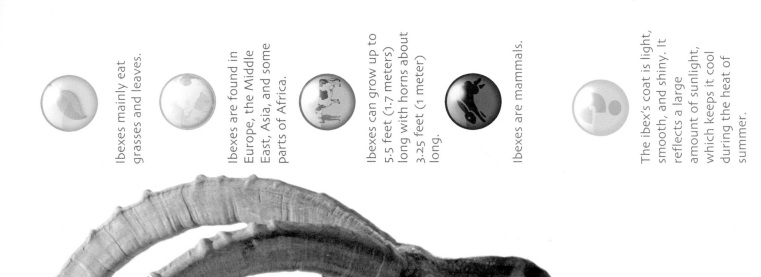

Ibex

Llama

Safari Sam says:
Llamas are very social herd animals.
Sometimes, they spit at each other
as a way of disciplining other
llamas in the herd.

Llamas

Llamas are domesticated animals that people living in the Andes Mountains use as pack animals. Llamas can carry up to 30 percent of their body weight. They also are farmed for their wool. Llamas have fine undercoat hair, which can be used to make clothing. Their coarser outer hair can be used to make rugs and ropes.

Llamas are related to camels.

Baby llamas are called "crias" from the Spanish word for "baby animal."

Llamas can grow up to 6 feet (1.8 meters) tall at the head and can weigh up to 450 pounds (200 kilograms).

Llamas live in the Andes Mountains of South America.

Llamas only eat plants.

Mountain Lions

Also known as cougars or pumas, mountain lions are powerful predators that roam North and South America.

They prey on deer and smaller animals, such as raccoons. They stalk their prey before leaping on them to deliver a killing bite to the neck.

Mountain lions eat deer, coyotes, raccoons, mice, squirrels, elk, wild pigs, porcupines, and beavers.

Mountain lions are found in many types of habitats throughout the Americas.

Mountain lions can grow to about 5 feet (1.5 meters) long, with a tail about 2.5 feet (0.76 meters) long.

Mountain lions are cats.

A mountain lion is able to leap as high as 15 feet (4.6 meters) in one bound. It can reach speeds of 50 mph (80 kph) when running.

Safari Sam says:
Like domestic cats, mountain lions have night vision and mainly hunt during the evening and at night.

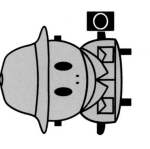

Mountain lion

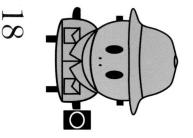

Pandas

The panda, or giant panda, lives in a few mountain ranges in central China. Its black and white fur is ideal camouflage in the snowy and rocky habitat. Pandas spend most of their time eating bamboo shoots.

Safari Sam says:
The giant panda can eat as much as 85 pounds (40 kilograms) of bamboo shoots per day.

The giant panda's diet is 99 percent bamboo. Occasionally, it will eat other grasses, wild tubers, birds, rodents, or dead animals.

Pandas live in bamboo forests in the mountain regions of central China.

Pandas measure about 6 feet (1.8 meter) long and can weigh about 300 pounds (140 kilograms).

Pandas are bears.

The giant panda has a thumb and five fingers.

Giant panda cub

Snow Leopards

These beautiful, big cats
live in snowy mountains.
Their thick, white fur
helps keeps them
warm and
camouflaged.
They hunt
wild sheep
and goats
at dawn
and at
dusk.

Safari Sam says:
Snow leopards can travel
on top of soft snow
because their large paws
work like snowshoes.
The paws are completely
covered in fur so that
they do not feel the cold.

Snow leopards feed on wild sheep and goats. They are also known to eat smaller animals, such as rodents, hares, and game birds.

Snow leopards are found in the high, rugged mountains of Central Asia.

Snow leopards grow up to 7.5 feet (2.3 meters), which includes a 3.3-foot (1-meter) tail length.

Snow leopards are cats.

Unlike most other big cats, snow leopards are unable to roar.

Snow leopard

Safari Sam says:
The yak can live at high altitudes because it has a larger heart and lungs than the cattle that live at lower altitudes. These organs allow the yak to absorb enough oxygen from the thin mountain air to live.

Yak

Yaks

The yak is a sturdy, cowlike animal that lives throughout the Himalayan region, where the world's highest mountains are found. The yak's extremely thick, long fur hangs down lower than their belly and helps keep them warm in the thin, cold air.

Yaks are **herbivores** and graze on vegetation, such as grasses growing in the mountains.

Yaks are found throughout the Himalayan region of south Central Asia, the Tibetan Plateau, and as far north as Mongolia and Russia.

Wild yaks are among the largest cowlike animals. They stand over 6 feet (1.8 meters) tall at the shoulder and weigh about 1,200 pounds (500 kilograms).

Yaks are mammals and are related to other animals with **cloven hooves,** including cattle.

In some countries in the Himalayas, yak racing is a popular form of entertainment at traditional festivals.

Glossary

carcass
The body of a dead animal.

cloven hooves
A hoof split into two toes.

herbivore
An animal that feeds only on plants.

rodent
A mammal with front teeth that continuously grow and are kept short by gnawing.

scavenger
An animal that feeds on the dead bodies of other animals.

Index